THE HEAD
OF A GREAT
LEADER

IT STARTS ON THE INSIDE

An in-depth study guide by

KEN BLANCHARD & PHIL HODGES
with STEVE GARDNER

LEAD LIKE JESUS

TABLE OF CONTENTS

OUR HOPE FOR YOU

WE WANT YOU TO EXPERIENCE JESUS IN A WHOLE DIFFERENT WAY — TO GROW TO TRUST HIM AS THE PERFECT ONE TO FOLLOW AS YOU SEEK TO LEAD OTHERS. THIS INVOLVES SURRENDERING OUR LIVES AND LEADERSHIP TO HIM.

The real secret to leading like Jesus is found in Proverbs 3:5-6: *Trust in the Lord with all your heart and lean not on your own understanding; in all your ways acknowledge him, and he will make your paths straight.*

Jesus is clear about how He wants us to lead. He asks us to make a difference in our world by being effective servant leaders. It is our prayer and desire that this Lead Like Jesus *Head Study Guide* will be the beginning of a new and exciting chapter in your personal journey to becoming just that. It is designed to guide you in exploring your personal response to Jesus' call to *follow Me* and to put into action the principles of servant leadership.

Don't worry if you do not have a formal leadership role. The principles are applicable to your relationship with your spouse, kids, friends, coworkers, colleagues, and casual acquaintances. This isn't the intellectual pursuit of a complicated philosophy of leadership; it is a guide to a more practical application of the truths of Scripture. We want you to think differently, but we also want you to develop a lifestyle that is built upon and governed by your relationship with Jesus Christ — the ultimate leader!

♥ 🖤 ✋ ↻

STUDY GUIDE OVERVIEW

HOW THIS STUDY GUIDE IS DESIGNED

We have designed this guide for daily study so that the principles you learn can be consistently put to work in your daily life. The focus is your head — your belief system and perspective on the role of the leader. As you are challenged to look at your own leadership, resist the temptation to respond in ways that you wish things were but do not actually reflect your current, up-to-now motivations, attitudes, actions, and beliefs. The truth of the moment may not be pretty. But Jesus said *"the truth will set you free"* (John 8:32) and so it will, when you confront it with honesty and the knowledge that, in Jesus, we have received the ultimate expression of God's unconditional love and forgiveness.

You will find the following icons throughout the text to guide your thinking:

MEMORY VERSE FOR THE WEEK Hiding God's Word in your heart is how you keep your way pure (Ps. 119). Take time each week to store this treasure in your heart and mind.

QUOTE OF THE TODAY A wise word to get us started in the right direction.

WHAT GOD'S WORD SAYS We will seek first the kingdom by God by looking to His Word as our source of wisdom and direction. When God's Word speaks specifically of how followers of Jesus are to walk a different path from the world around them in heart, mind, body, and spirit, we will seek not to ask *why*, but rather *how*.

PAUSE AND REFLECT This is an opportunity to consider the proposed concept and to record your reaction to it.

A PRAYER FOR TODAY Following in the habit of Jesus, we will make prayer our first response instead of our last resort. As we invite the Holy Spirit to guide our thoughts, we will take time to read the prayer for the day and offer it up to God as our own.

TODAY'S TOPIC Segments adapted and expanded from *Lead Like Jesus: Lessons from the Greatest Leadership Role Model of All Time*, a book by Ken Blanchard and Phil Hodges on which this study guide is based.

LOOK INSIDE Through the use of a variety of learning tools, questionnaires, and exercises, we will explore our *up-to-now* leadership motivations, thinking, behavior, and habits and how they compare with leading like Jesus.

★ **KEY CONCEPTS** As we explore leading like Jesus, we will discover key principles, concepts, and nonnegotiable mandates that we are not able to accomplish on our own but are called to implement under the guidance of the Holy Spirit.

♀ **A POINT TO PONDER** A thought or idea to keep with us throughout the day.

✈ **NEXT STEPS** *Leading like Jesus* will be a lifetime journey to be traveled in His company step-by-step, moment-by-moment. At the end of each day's lesson, you will be asked to prayerfully consider your Next Steps.

HOW CAN YOU REAP THE GREATEST BENEFITS FROM THIS STUDY?

1. Pray for insight each day as you meet the Lord through this study. Let Him lead you to experience His direction in your life through every learning activity.

2. Experience the focus for each day as you study and apply it to your life. Write down those Aha! ideas that challenge your leadership behaviors and motives. Ask yourself how you can realign your leadership to better reflect Christ's example.

3. Review your progress each week and recognize what God is doing in your life and in the lives of those you lead.

4. Keep a journal in which you will list the action steps and plans associated with your Aha! ideas. Additionally, write down specific ways in which you are putting into practice what you are learning.

5. As your group follows the instructions in the Facilitator's Guide found at **www.LeadLikeJesus. com/FreeStuff**, your knowledge of the principles and their application to everyday life will be multiplied. You cannot learn to lead like Jesus unless you interact with other people. If a small group study isn't possible, invite one or two other people to go through the study with you.

We hope as you learn to trust Jesus as your leadership model, it will make you an active agent for restoring joy to work and family. So whether you're leading in business, nonprofit organizations, your community, your church, or your home, you will make Jesus smile. It is the vision of the Lead Like Jesus ministry (**LeadLikeJesus.com**) that … that someday, everyone, everywhere will be impacted by someone leading like Jesus.

A POINT TO PONDER

Imagine this setting: You, Jesus, and the authors of this *Study Guide* are sitting together conversing about His kind of leadership. Just as the Master Teacher did with His disciples, you will be asked questions, given assignments, and told stories and examples that will help you connect your own experiences with leading like Jesus. So, as you interact with this study guide, invite the Holy Spirit to guide you to new insights and a new perspective on how to put what you learn into practice. Together we will learn to lead like Jesus!

LEAD LIKE JESUS

3506 Professional Circle, Suite B
Augusta, GA 30907
800.383.6890

LeadLikeJesus.com

WE HAVE ALL SEEN LEADERS, IN CORPORATE AMERICA, EXPLOIT PRIVILEGES OF POSITION BRINGING RUIN TO EMPLOYEES AND INVESTORS.

Meanwhile citizens of under-developed countries languish in poverty and hopelessness in a leadership vacuum. At the same time all across the country, the witness and ministry of churches are compromised and stymied by a crisis of integrity in their leaders. In stark contrast to the failures and foibles of 21st Century leadership stands the perfect leadership role model – **Jesus of Nazareth**.

Lead Like Jesus, a 501 (c)(3) organization, co-founded in 1999, by Ken Blanchard, co-author of **The One Minute Manager**, and his longtime friend, Phil Hodges imagines a world in which leaders serve rather than rule, a world in which they give rather than take. We imagine leaders who seek to produce results from service and sacrifice rather than from power and position. We recognize this only happens as leaders adopt Jesus as their leadership role model and grow in His likeness.

We exist to help leaders of all shapes, sizes, ages and aspirations to explore and express the leadership principles Jesus lived. To that end we are both humbled and honored to be entrusted with the stewardship of this vision that "someday, everyone, everywhere will be impacted by someone leading like Jesus."

In **Matthew 20**, Jesus expressed His view of leadership in His *Not So With You* mandate. This principle is a driving force of **Lead Like Jesus**.

For more information on **Lead Like Jesus** or it's programs, services and events, visit **www.LeadLikeJesus.com**

♥ 👤 ✋ ↻

A LETTER FROM PHYLLIS

Dear Reader,

It is with great excitement that I invite you to dive deep into the Great Leader Study Guides. Jesus knew we would want to be great, so He told us how, with a clear directive that teaches us that greatness comes through service. In fact, servant leadership is the only approach to leadership Jesus ever validates for His followers.

It sounds simple, but serving others does not come easily or naturally. Behavior that demonstrates service comes from a heart that has been transformed by love through a deep connection to the Father. The result is thinking that is others-centered and behavior that seeks to serve. The Great Leader Study Guides were created to help people dig deeper into four areas of growth: The Heart, Head, Hands, and Habits. Our desire is to help you, as a follower of Jesus, reflect Him more and more in every situation, with those you influence.

I pray that out of His glorious riches He may strengthen you with power through His Spirit in your inner being, so that Christ may dwell in your hearts through faith. And I pray that you, being rooted and established in love, may have power, together with all the saints, to grasp how wide and long and high and deep is the love of Christ, and to know this love that surpasses knowledge — that you may be filled to the measure of all the fullness of God.
EPHESIANS 3:16-19

Amen!

Praying for you,

Phyllis H. Hendry
President & CEO
Lead Like Jesus

WEEK ONE
GET YOUR HEAD ON THE RIGHT TRACK

MEMORY VERSE FOR THE WEEK

Do not conform any longer to the pattern of this world, but be transformed by there newing of your mind. Then you will be able to test and approve what God's will is — his good, pleasing and perfect will.

ROMANS 12:2

Every leader is also a follower. Your leadership perspective — how you see your role and your relationship to those you are influencing — progressively reflects the person you hold up as a model. When that person is Jesus, you experience ongoing transformation that takes you ever further from the pattern of this world.

We all know the pattern of this world when it comes to leadership. It's the natural tendency to lord it over others in the self-serving exercise of authority (Matthew 20:25). But when Jesus is your leader, you don't shrug off His clear mandate: *Not so with you. Instead, whoever wants to become great among you must be your servant* (MATTHEW 20:26).

Some leadership choices are obvious, requiring nothing more than discipline. Others require the ability to test and approve what God's will is. This is the domain of a transformed mind — the head of a Jesus follower.

GET YOUR **HEAD** ON THE RIGHT TRACK
KNOWLEDGE IS ONLY THE BEGINNING

99 QUOTE FOR TODAY

The overarching truth about leading like Jesus is that it can only be accomplished by continuing to walk closer and closer to Him in a surrendered relationship of trust and love.
KEN BLANCHARD AND PHIL HODGES

WHAT GOD'S WORD SAYS

Give me wisdom and knowledge, that I may lead this people.
2 CHRONICLES 1:10

And Jesus grew in wisdom.
LUKE 2:52

PAUSE AND REFLECT

Do you have any idea what percentage of your knowledge translates into productive action? Half? Twenty-five percent? Ten percent? One percent? Even if we narrow the question to consider only "actionable knowledge," the percentage is likely to be embarrassingly low. Some of us are so good at rationalizing that we fail to see how often our problem is not one of knowledge but rather one of will. Can you identify any examples of this in your recent past?

_____

_____

_____

_____

A PRAYER FOR TODAY

Lord, thank You for the ability to comprehend and learn. Thank You for *wisdom and knowledge* that I can internalize. Help me to be quick to apply the truth You reveal to me. I don't want to just know about You; I want to know You and to walk in a surrendered relationship of trust and love. In Jesus' name, Amen!

☀ TODAY'S TOPIC

If we didn't believe in the importance of knowledge, we wouldn't spend time and energy teaching principles of leadership. But knowledge is only potential; it doesn't have tangible value until it is put into play.

Consider the example of Solomon. His request for wisdom and knowledge to lead God's people is commendable, shown by God's response in 2 Chronicles 1:11-12. Unfortunately, Solomon's good intentions failed to prevent his love of knowledge from outstripping his willingness to apply it — at least when it came to heeding God's specific warnings.

The king, moreover, must not acquire great numbers of horses for himself or make the people return to Egypt to get more of them, for the Lord has told you, 'You are not to go back that way again.' He must not take many wives, or his heart will be led astray. He must not accumulate large amounts of silver and gold (DEUTERONOMY 17:16-17).

Three very direct prohibitions; three equally direct violations (see 2 Chronicles 1:14-17; 1 Kings 11:1-5). Solomon's wisdom led to enormous success; his departure from it led to disaster. Wisdom can never be divorced from obedience to God's revealed will.

Jesus certainly knew more than any of us ever will, but He never placed His confidence in mere knowledge. We like to say it this way: Data is not information. Information is not knowledge. Knowledge is not wisdom. Wisdom is connecting all of these with God's purposes. It is truth and obedience combined, and Jesus modeled it perfectly.

💼 LOOK INSIDE

"Whoever acquires knowledge and does not practice it resembles him who plows his land and leaves it unsown." GULISTAN (1258) How do you evaluate the fruitfulness of your leadership studies? Are you planting, watering and weeding so that the plowed ground is producing a return?

_____

_____

_____

THE HEAD OF A GREAT LEADER

★ KEY CONCEPT

Truth becomes productive wisdom only when it is connected with God's purposes and coupled with sustained obedience.

💡 A POINT TO PONDER

"Your intelligence has gotten you into this," the counselor frequently told our friend. When intelligence thinks it can outsmart wisdom — truth and obedience combined — it must bear the consequences. And when intelligence results in increased power, the consequences also increase. Satan was the first to fail this test. Jesus, our model, was the first to pass it.

✈ NEXT STEPS

Could you be following Solomon's example, somehow rationalizing ventures into areas God has prohibited? Sometimes we are tempted to ask, "What harm is there in this?" As though God might prohibit something beneficial. Asking the question is fine — as long as we are committed to the superiority of His perspective over ours. In what areas do you risk an erosion of obedience?

_____

_____

_____

Where then does wisdom come from? Where does understanding dwell? And he [God] said to man, 'The fear of the Lord — that is wisdom, and to shun evil is understanding' (JOB 28:20, 28). As you begin this study, list three actions you can take to protect yourself from following Solomon's example. As a starting point, consider Jesus' responses to Satan's direct temptations in Matthew 4:1-10.

_____

_____

WILL YOU HIRE JESUS?

WEEK 1

DAY 2

99 QUOTE FOR TODAY

Excellence demands that you be better than yourself.
TED ENGSTROM

WHAT GOD'S WORD SAYS

In the beginning was the Word, and the Word was with God, and the Word was God ... Through him all things were made ... The Word became flesh and made his dwelling among us. We have seen his glory, the glory of the One and Only, who came from the Father, full of grace and truth.
JOHN 1:1, 3, 14

And Jesus grew in wisdom ...
LUKE 2:52

❙❙ PAUSE AND REFLECT

After reading these verses that introduce Jesus, take a few minutes to reflect on the implications of who He is. How would you evaluate His educational qualifications?

_____

_____

What about His network — significant contacts?_____

_____

What about His balance — (full of grace and truth)?_____

_____

A PRAYER FOR TODAY

Lord, thank You for Jesus. Thank You for His wisdom, power, and grace. Thank You for the time He spent walking this planet and leading imperfect people — people like me — to help them see and know You. I want to know You better. Help me to lead like Jesus as I lead myself and others. In Jesus' name, Amen!

☀ TODAY'S TOPIC

Let's get something straight right up front. Jesus is our leadership role model. In case you're wondering why, let us assure you that we haven't chosen Him because it's a good religious thing to do. Nor have we made Him our model so we could subtly bring God into leadership literature.

We have chosen Jesus as our leadership role model simply because He is the greatest leader who ever lived. Consider this list of credentials:

1. Led an imperfect team of problem people

2. Took time to train and develop them, delegating authority in the process

3. Passed constant scrutiny and testing of commitment and integrity

4. Handled criticism, opposition and rejection with power under control

5. Faced fierce competition and conflicting demands — even from friends

6. Endured intense temptation of instant gratification, recognition, and misuse of power

7. Faced serious personnel issues including betrayal and defection under pressure

8. Communicated effectively in a multicultural environment

9. Challenged the status quo and hierarchy to bring about change

10. Communicated a radically new vision, calling people to sacrifice for it

11. Remained faithful to the mission regardless of career consequences

Our question, "Will you hire Jesus?" is not meant to be disrespectful. We just want to show in very practical terms that He would be the greatest consultant you could ever imagine. Once you make that connection, you can begin to study His leadership perspective and effectiveness. As the greatest leader who ever lived, He is worth following.

💼 LOOK INSIDE

As you consider the list of 11 leadership credentials we've noted above, none of them should be irrelevant to you and your leadership situation. Which would you choose as your current top three areas of need?

1. _____

2. _____

3. _____

★ KEY CONCEPT

Every leader needs outside help, and Jesus is without peer as a leader to follow and a model to emulate.

○ A POINT TO PONDER

Have you ever found yourself in a mess and been wise enough to realize that your ignorance or stubbornness or arrogance got you there? Chances are you haven't thought — or been told as the friend we mentioned yesterday was — "Your intelligence has gotten you into this."

Our friend thought he was smart enough to figure things out on his own. But he wasn't. Because although intelligence is a good thing, it's not enough. Like any other power tool, it can be useless — or even destructive — if it's not used in the right way. But in the hands of a master ...

Are you ready to surrender your intelligence to the Master? Are you ready to gain His perspective on life and leadership?

◁ NEXT STEPS

Imagine yourself responding to an invitation for leadership mentoring with Jesus. What practical things would you hope to learn from Him? Write a brief request that outlines the needs you would like to address.

_____

_____

_____

_____

TRUSTING JESUS' LEADERSHIP

QUOTE FOR TODAY

Believe me when I say that I am in the Father and the Father is in me; or at least believe on the evidence of the miracles themselves.
JOHN 14:11

WHAT GOD'S WORD SAYS

Greater love has no one than this, that he lay down his life for his friends. You are my friends if you do what I command. I no longer call you servants, because a servant does not know his master's business. Instead, I have called you friends, for everything that I learned from my Father I have made known to you. You did not choose me, but I chose you and appointed you to go and bear fruit — fruit that will last. Then the Father will give you whatever you ask in my name.
JOHN 15:13-16

PAUSE AND REFLECT

When you think of the people who have had the most positive influence on you in face-to-face relationships, how would you rate your level of trust in them?

Low --Complete

     1   2   3   4   5

What did they do that built trust in you?

_____

_____

_____

A PRAYER FOR TODAY

Lord, You know the disappointments I've experienced that sometimes make me reluctant to trust. Please free me from my prison of unbelief so I can receive and act on Your power. And as I learn to trust You more fully, help me to be trustworthy and build trust in those who follow me. In Jesus' name, Amen!

☀ TODAY'S TOPIC

A study of historic leadership uncovers all kinds of leaders. Some have risen to global dominance based on psychological manipulation and the use of raw power. That kind of leadership inevitably comes to a violent end, because it relies on fear rather than trust.

Jesus takes the opposite approach. Because His goal is to serve and develop followers rather than use them selfishly, He works from a trust base rather than a power base. Much of what He says to us is designed to build our trust in Him. Sometimes He says it directly by saying "Believe Me; I am telling you the truth."

Other times He says it between the lines as in the John 15 passage on page 18. Even when it is between the lines, it permeates the message as surely as if he had stated it this way:

1. Trust Me: I care about you — enough to lay down My life for you.

2. Trust Me: I am transforming you from servants to friends.

3. Trust Me: I know what I am doing. Everything that I learned from My Father …

4. Trust Me: I am trusting you … I have made known to you.

5. Trust Me: I am for you. I chose you.

6. Trust Me: I will give you results. I have appointed you to bear fruit that will last.

7. Trust Me: I will give you My resources. The Father will give you whatever you ask in My name.

💼 LOOK INSIDE

How much do you trust Jesus' leadership? Is He worthy of more trust than you are giving? How can you move in the direction of taking Him at His word?

_____

_____

_____

_____

★ KEY CONCEPT

Nothing is more empowering than a relationship built on the trust Jesus deserves and to which He calls us.

A POINT TO PONDER

As a leader, you cannot expect trust that exceeds your trustworthiness.

NEXT STEPS

1. Meditate on John 15:13-16 and its implications for your trust in Jesus' leadership.

2. How can you use His example in your family, church, community or organization?

TO LEAD IS TO FOLLOW IS TO OBEY

" QUOTE FOR TODAY

There is one perfect leadership role model you can trust, and His name is Jesus.
KEN BLANCHARD AND PHIL HODGES

WHAT GOD'S WORD SAYS

I do nothing on my own but speak just what the Father has taught me.
JOHN 8:28

❚❚ PAUSE AND REFLECT

Have you ever thought about the fact that Jesus, the world's all-time greatest leader, was a follower Himself? What was His pattern as a follower?

1. How does Mark 1:35 describe His followership?

2. How does Mark 14:35-36 describe His followership?

3. How does John 15:10 describe His followership?

4. What are the implications for our followership?

_____

_____

_____

A PRAYER FOR TODAY

Lord, thank You for providing Jesus as a model of both leadership and followership. Help me to yield my natural tendency to choose independence over obedience. Thank You for the invitation to remain in Your love and to experience complete joy. In Jesus' name, Amen!

☼ TODAY'S TOPIC

Everyone knows that leaders want obedient followers; it makes getting the job done so much easier. But not everyone realizes that effective leaders are also followers. In fact, they have risen to their position after first learning the discipline of obedient followership.

Followership without obedience is an oxymoron. Lack of obedience means lack of alignment and, of necessity, going in an independent direction. This condition, rooted in pride, was Satan's downfall. It is also ours. Jesus, however, consistently avoided this temptation. He chose constant obedience and remained in perfect alignment.

Because Jesus fully aligned Himself with God's instructions, He had God's point of view. His early-morning prayer time (Mark 1:35) gave Him His marching orders for the day — in this case, a very counterintuitive strategy. He left the ready-made crowd to go where He was yet unknown. ... *Let us go somewhere else — to the nearby villages — so I can preach there also. That is why I have come* (MARK 1:38).

Did you notice the last sentence? *That is why I have come.* Alignment with God's instructions leads to God's point of view and clarity of purpose.

Jesus knew He could not remain aligned with the Father's instructions without being in constant, intimate relationship with the Father. It was the only way He could pass the ultimate test of His leadership. Golgotha was looming somewhere in His future, and although He had fully signed on to the plan, He knew the cost-benefit ratio would not look the same on this side of the human divide.

Intimacy with the Father was an absolute necessity. No Gethsemane, no Golgotha. No Golgotha, no victory.

💼 LOOK INSIDE

Are you fully aligned with God's instructions? Have you discovered the link between obeying and remaining in intimate relationship with the Father? How are you living out John 15:10?

_____

_____

_____

★ KEY CONCEPT

Every leader is also a follower, gaining power through obedience to a higher authority.

♡ A POINT TO PONDER

Jesus' earthly life as a follower required trusting the Father and living by faith — just as ours does.

◁ NEXT STEPS

Put your followership to the test. Jesus said, *My command is this: Love each other as I have loved you. Greater love has no one than this, that he lay down his life for his friends* (JOHN 15:12-13). List two or three ways you presently obey this command.

_____

_____

_____

_____

Ask God to open a door to a new way of living out Jesus' command — not necessarily new in the sense of something that's never been done before but something you're not currently doing or doing well. Wait quietly for a few minutes to see what He reveals. Jot down your thoughts and watch expectantly for opportunities to act.

_____

_____

_____

_____

GET YOUR **HEAD** ON THE RIGHT TRACK
U-TURN POWER

" QUOTE FOR TODAY

"Leaders should be the chief repenters."
JACK MILLER

WHAT GOD'S WORD SAYS

... I know that you acted in ignorance, as did your leaders. ... Repent, then, and turn to God, so that your sins may be wiped out, that times of refreshing may come from the Lord.
ACTS 3:17, 19

❚❚ PAUSE AND REFLECT

How many times have you made a wrong turn and tried to rectify it by a convoluted combination of parallel routes and angles? You may have rationalized that it would save time or be more direct, but the refusal to make a simple U-turn was probably more about pride than efficiency.

The one thing you didn't do was just keep going in what you knew was the wrong direction. Have you ever seen a leader just keep going, driven by ego or greed? What did (or would) you think of such a leader?

_____

_____

_____

_____

🙏 A PRAYER FOR TODAY

Lord, thank You for Your promise to wipe out my sins when I repent and turn back to You. Thank You for the vision of times of refreshing that await me. Help me to have the wisdom and humility to make quick and direct U-turns when I get off track. In Jesus' name, Amen!

☀ TODAY'S TOPIC

When our followers get out of alignment, we want a course correction — and we want it now. Often we can spot misalignment even when those following insist it isn't there. We recognize that many things, including competing commitments, may distort their perspective.

One of the most important jobs of a leader is defining reality for those who follow. Often, however, the brutal facts require addressing our own errors: a mistake in judgment, an ill-conceived strategy or even a good strategy that has run its course and outlived its usefulness. The facts defining our reality indicate that a U-turn is needed.

We know that mistakes in execution are unavoidable, but we have a hard time accepting mistakes in planning or strategy. Harder yet is admitting that pride or selfishness or fear have overtaken our diligence in following Jesus. As long as circumstances seem to cooperate, we are tempted to delay a strategic U-turn.

Once it is clear that a turn is needed, there is no gain in putting it off or trying to finesse it. The sooner, the better — especially when the mistakes involve wandering from the path mandated by Jesus. *Those whom I love I rebuke and discipline. So be earnest, and repent* (REVELATION 3:19).

Paul's commendation of the Corinthians' repentance is just as appropriate for us today. ... *I am happy, not because you were made sorry, but because your sorrow led you to repentance. For you became sorrowful as God intended ... Godly sorrow brings repentance that leads to salvation and leaves no regret ...* (2 CORINTHIANS 7:9-10).

This is the kind of sorrow and repentance we want — a U-turn that returns us to following Jesus, to getting back into alignment with God's plan for us.

💼 LOOK INSIDE

How does today's quote, "Leaders should be the chief repenters" strike you? Hopefully, you're not a leader who thinks repentance is something to be delegated.

_____

_____

_____

★ KEY CONCEPT

Our disobedience has consequences: emotional pain and sometimes even physical illness. There is only one remedy: repentance on our part and complete forgiveness on His.

💡 A POINT TO PONDER

Repentance usually includes Godly sorrow, but it's not primarily about the sorrow; it's about the change in direction. There is no repentance without a U-turn.

✈ NEXT STEPS

O Lord, you have searched me and you know me. You know when I sit and when I rise; you perceive my thoughts from afar. You discern my going out and my lying down; you are familiar with all my ways. Before a word is on my tongue you know it completely, O Lord (PSALM 139:1-4).

Since nothing is hidden from God, and since the only unforgivable sin is refusing to acknowledge Him and repent, why would you not want to be a "chief repenter?"

_____

_____

_____

_____

Thank God for placing unlimited U-turn opportunities along your path. Unload your sin burden, and ask God to reveal to you anything else He knows is weighing you down. *Search me, O God, and know my heart; test me and know my anxious thoughts. See if there is any offensive way in me, and lead me in the way everlasting* (PSALM 139:23-24).

_____

_____

_____

_____

WEEK TWO
TRANSFORMATIONAL LEADERSHIP CYCLE

MEMORY VERSE FOR THE WEEK

And Jesus grew in wisdom and stature, and in favor with God and men.
LUKE 2:52

... Everyone who is fully trained will be like his teacher.
LUKE 6:40

The leadership journey begins where you are now, and it begins on the inside. To lead like Jesus means to follow the same pattern He followed in developing His leadership.

Jesus first learned to lead Himself. This first step can be extremely challenging, and there is no shortcut. We see part of this played out in Matthew 3:13-4:11. The temptations He faced in the wilderness — His direct face-to-face encounter with Satan — are beyond anything you will ever face, but yours will probably feel as intense to you.

Then in Matthew 4:18-24 we see Jesus begin one-on-one leadership as He calls individuals to follow Him and leads them in the personal growth they will need in their role as His disciples.

Next we see Jesus in team leadership. Matthew 10:5-10 shows Him instructing and equipping His team of twelve to go out into the community to preach, heal, and do miracles.

Finally, in Matthew 28:19-20, we see Jesus in organizational leadership as He is establishing His church by sending His fully trained disciples to change the world.

Your progression as a leader follows a similar path. And remember that it is a repeating cycle; you never outgrow the need to lead yourself or to lead individuals one-on-one regardless of how large an organization you may someday lead.

TRANSFORMATIONAL LEADERSHIP CYCLE
WHO LEADS AND WHO FOLLOWS?

" QUOTE FOR TODAY

Learning to lead like Jesus is more than an announcement; it is a commitment to lead in a different way.

KEN BLANCHARD AND PHIL HODGES

WHAT GOD'S WORD SAYS

You are the light of the world. A city on a hill cannot be hidden. Neither do people light a lamp and put it under a bowl. Instead they put it on its stand, and it gives light to everyone in the house. In the same way, let your light shine before men, that they may see your good deeds and praise your Father in heaven.

MATTHEW 5:14-16

❙❙ PAUSE AND REFLECT

Consider what Jesus is saying to His followers in these three verses. Are you a light in your world? If so, God will not allow you to remain hidden; He will orchestrate events in such a way that your light is seen.

Some people get more concerned about their placement than about giving light. That's backward. God will lead others to decide what stand we are fit for and place us there in due time if we let our light shine where we are now. Are you being faithful with your light? Describe where it is shining and what difference it is making.

_____

_____

_____

_____

🙏 A PRAYER FOR TODAY

Lord, thank You for giving me the desire to lead. Help me to get it right, to lead for the right reasons and to lead like Jesus did — for Your glory. I want to be a light in the world so that people will know and praise You. As You increase my responsibility and my platform, help me to keep my eyes focused on You. In Jesus' name, Amen!

☼ TODAY'S TOPIC

Leadership naturally begins by learning to lead yourself. Then, as the Transformational Leadership Cycle diagram shows, it naturally expands to ever-increasing public leadership.

In talking about money and values, Jesus describes a parallel principle when He says, *"Whoever can be trusted with very little can also be trusted with much, and whoever is dishonest with very little will also be dishonest with much"* (LUKE 16:10). Early leadership opportunities handled faithfully pave the way for larger ones.

Read carefully through the diagram, including the referenced Scriptures, to get an overview of how Jesus progressed in His own leadership. This is the same way we progress.

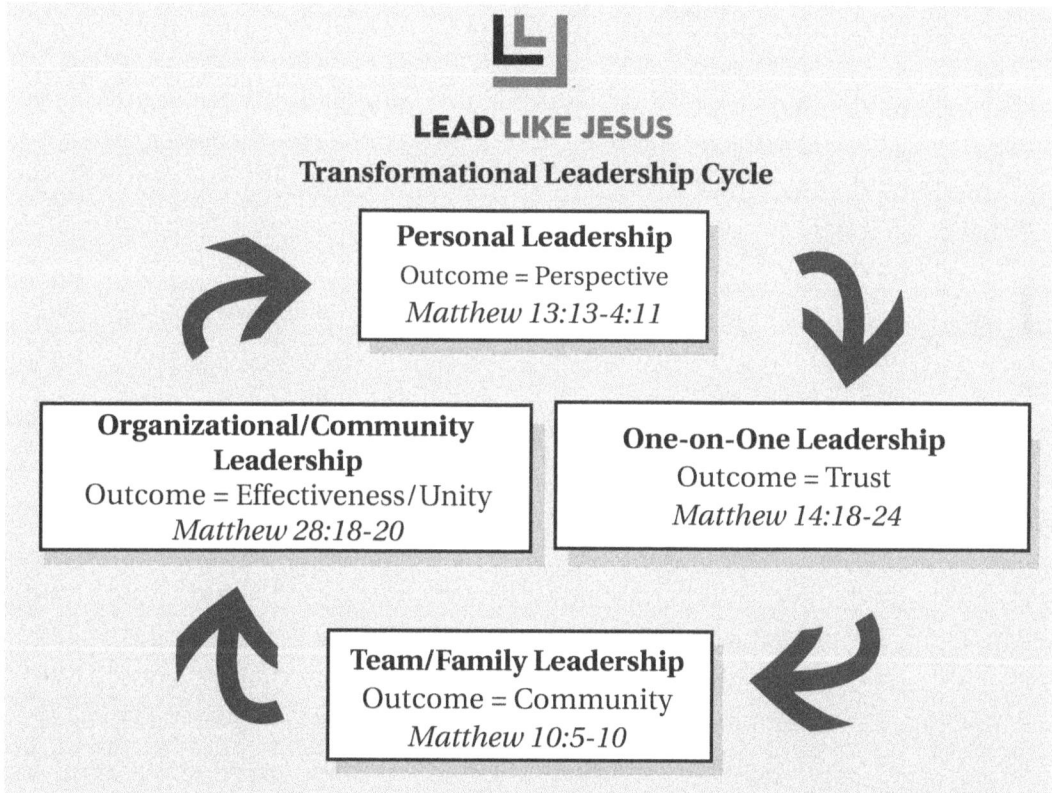

LEAD LIKE JESUS
Transformational Leadership Cycle

Personal Leadership
Outcome = Perspective
Matthew 13:13-4:11

Organizational/Community Leadership
Outcome = Effectiveness/Unity
Matthew 28:18-20

One-on-One Leadership
Outcome = Trust
Matthew 14:18-24

Team/Family Leadership
Outcome = Community
Matthew 10:5-10

💼 LOOK INSIDE

Where would you place yourself in the diagram? At what level(s) are you currently leading?.

_____

_____

_____

⭐ KEY CONCEPT

Leadership grows from inside out, from private to public, from smaller to larger.

💡 A POINT TO PONDER

Have you ever desired to start at the top? Don't worry; it's normal. But that doesn't make it right. Nor does it work that way. It's okay to have great ambitions — they may even be God-given. Just don't let them get ahead of Jesus in your priorities or timetable.

✈ NEXT STEPS

Thinking of your current level of leadership, list three specific actions you could take to let your light shine more brightly.

_____

_____

_____

_____

_____

_____

99 QUOTE FOR TODAY

No man is fit to command another that cannot command himself.
WILLIAM PENN

WHAT GOD'S WORD SAYS

For the Lord God is a sun and shield; the Lord bestows favor and honor; no good thing does he withhold from those whose walk is blameless.
PSALM 84:11

Do you not know that your body is a temple of the Holy Spirit, who is in you, whom you have received from God? You are not your own; you were bought at a price. Therefore honor God with your body.
1 CORINTHIANS 6:19-20

▌▌ PAUSE AND REFLECT

Have you ever seen someone who was quick to tell everyone else what to do in spite of lacking the discipline to do it himself? Unfortunately, we all have. And it doesn't work.

How would you describe your level of personal leadership at this point? Do you live a life that is surrendered to God's Spirit living within you?

Unsurrendered --Surrendered
1   2   3   4   5

Are you committed to values that are in line with God's character? Do you consistently model the behaviors you want from those who will follow you? Jot your honest thoughts and feelings about these questions.

_____

_____

🙏 A PRAYER FOR TODAY

Lord, thank You for placing Your Spirit in me to help me do what I can't do in my own strength. I want to grow in my trust and quickness to surrender to Your Spirit. Help me remember that You withhold no good thing and that Your way is always best. In Jesus' name, Amen!!

☀ TODAY'S TOPIC

Even Jesus, God in flesh, did not begin public ministry without personal preparation. Fortunately, Matthew 3:13-4:11 gives us a peek into some of His personal leadership. His baptism and subsequent temptation in the wilderness combine to answer two pivotal questions that we must also answer:

1. **Whose am I?** Who is my primary authority? Who am I trying to please? Regardless of humanity's natural desire to be self-centered and focused on temporal values, there is only one correct answer for any follower of Christ. We belong to God. Our bodies are not our own. We are here to honor and glorify Him. The commitment to *seek first his kingdom and his righteousness* (MATTHEW 6:33) runs counter to the world's leadership. This single commitment, as simple as it seems, forms the basis for every struggle we face in life.

2. **Who am I?** Let's answer this at two levels: a) the identity you share with every other follower of Christ, and b) the identity God designed uniquely for you.

    a) *See how very much our Father loves us, for he calls us his children, and that is what we are! But the people who belong to this world don't recognize that we are God's children because they don't know him. Dear friends, we are already God's children, but he has not yet shown us what we will be like when Christ appears. But we do know that we will be like him, for we will see him as he really is. And all who have this eager expectation will keep themselves pure, just as he is pure* (1 JOHN 3:1-3 NLT).

    b) You are ... *God's workmanship, created in Christ Jesus to do good works, which God prepared in advance ...* (EPHESIANS 2:10). Although this is also true for every believer, your specific workmanship (DNA, personality, life experience, etc.) is unique — as are the good works prepared in advance for you to do. God designed you like no other, and His plans for your life are good.

💼 LOOK INSIDE

Until your highest priority is to glorify God by living within His identity for you, you are not leading yourself. This is not a one-time decision or a victory you achieve that then allows you to live on autopilot. This is a daily surrender, taking up your cross and dying to the ego-centric desires that simultaneously appeal and destroy.

How are you currently answering the "Whose am I?" and the "Who am I?" questions of personal leadership?

_____

_____

_____

★ KEY CONCEPT

Leading like Jesus begins at the personal level of recognizing that we are God's and must live for Him.

○ A POINT TO PONDER

In surrendering everything to God, we sacrifice our temporary illusions for His eternal reality.

◁ NEXT STEPS

Understanding that God has placed His Spirit in you to help you do what would be impossible in your own strength, list three commitments you believe would exemplify living to glorify God

1. _____

_____

_____

2. _____

_____

_____

3. _____

_____

_____

TRANSFORMATIONAL LEADERSHIP CYCLE
ONE-ON-ONE LEADERSHIP

" QUOTE FOR TODAY

Without trust, it is impossible for any organization to function effectively. Trust is a stream with a fragile ecological balance; once it is polluted, it will take time and effort to restore.
KEN BLANCHARD AND PHIL HODGES

WHAT GOD'S WORD SAYS

Therefore, if you are offering your gift at the altar and there remember that your brother has something against you, leave your gift there in front of the altar. First go and be reconciled to your brother; then come and offer your gift.
MATTHEW 5:23-24

So in everything, do to others what you would have them do to you ...
MATTHEW 7:12

PAUSE AND REFLECT

Do you see the connection between these verses and the trust you need to establish in any effective leadership relationship? In the Matthew 5 verses, Jesus describes a U-turn, a setting aside of pride to act with humble integrity in reconciling an estranged brother (spouse, child, peer, subordinate, etc.). This builds trust by showing yourself trustworthy. And when you have a habit of trustworthiness, it is much easier for you to trust others.

Anyone who strives to live by the Golden Rule (Matthew 7:12) is a natural trust builder.

_____

_____

_____

_____

A PRAYER FOR TODAY

Lord, thank You for the privilege of growing in leadership. And thank You for making trust something I can choose to earn and give — that it's not some kind of talent available only to the gifted. Help me to become thoroughly trustworthy as I lean on You. In Jesus' name, Amen

☼ TODAY'S TOPIC

Once you have life in proper perspective through self-examination, you can develop a trusting relationship with others. And trust is necessary — even for a group of two. Please remember this: If you revert to self-serving leadership, you will find people moving away from you rather than toward you.

We naturally want to put our best foot forward, even when it doesn't represent the rest of us. We tend to pose and hide, posture and deflect in the hope that others will find us acceptable — or better yet, admirable. And we deceive ourselves into thinking that others see only what we choose to present, that our hiddenness protects us from the rejection we would face if the awful truth were known.

Jesus had strong language for that phony kind of leadership. *You're hopeless, you religion scholars and Pharisees! Frauds! You're like manicured grave plots, grass clipped and the flowers bright, but six feet down it's all rotting bones and worm-eaten flesh. People look at you and think you're saints, but beneath the skin you're total frauds* (MATTHEW 23:27-28 MSG).

It takes transparency to sustain trust. It takes giving and receiving grace. It takes vulnerability. All of these qualities rely on humility, recognizing my need for God and others. This is not a difficult-to-grasp concept; it simply requires us to constantly monitor our self-serving tendency.

To admit mistakes, to repent, to reconcile, to look inward when we want to blame and outward to give credit, to keep confidences, to protect and defend teammates, to be first in line when sacrifice is needed, to live by the Golden Rule — all of these are trust builders, indispensable to anyone who aspires to lead like Jesus.

💼 LOOK INSIDE

How open are you with your close teammates regarding your challenges to live by the values you profess? Are you building and maintaining pockets of grace in a judgment-oriented world? Who can you honestly say knows the worst about you?

_____

_____

_____

_____

★ KEY CONCEPT

Leading like Jesus at the one-on-one level is about creating and sustaining trusting relationships

💡 A POINT TO PONDER

How did Jesus demonstrate giving trust? Was Peter trustworthy? Was he willing to stand up and be counted in Jesus' darkest hour? In spite of Peter's shameful failure — even after being forewarned — Jesus later tracked him down and re-commissioned him (John 21). This is trust, not driven by a proven track record but by grace, and in full recognition of what the Spirit could accomplish through Peter. And through you.

Are you willing to extend that kind of trust to those following you?

✈ NEXT STEPS

Look at the three commitments you listed in yesterday's Next Steps. How do they play out in one-on-one leadership? Write some thoughts about how each one will be seen by those closest to you

1. _____
   _____
   _____

2. _____
   _____
   _____

3. _____
   _____
   _____

QUOTE FOR TODAY

Failure to empower is one of the key reasons that teams are ineffective. [Team members] will not empower each other ... if they do not trust each other.
KEN BLANCHARD AND PHIL HODGES

WHAT GOD'S WORD SAYS

[Jesus] said, "Then you see how every student well-trained in God's kingdom is like the owner of a general store who can put his hands on anything you need, old or new, exactly when you need it."
MATTHEW 13:52 (MSG)

[Jesus] said to them, "Therefore every teacher of the law who has been instructed about the kingdom of heaven is like the owner of a house who brings out of his storeroom new treasures as well as old."
MATTHEW 13:52 (NIV)

PAUSE AND REFLECT

These two translations of Matthew 13:52 give us an interesting contrast in terms of the main character. One pictures him as a small business owner — a team leader — while the other pictures him as a homeowner — a family leader. Both show him being resourceful, a trusted equipper and provider of value. *If this is the kind of team/family leader you want to be, pay attention to the qualifier Jesus sets up: every student well-trained in God's kingdom.* What do you need to do to satisfy this qualifier?

_____

_____

_____

_____

A PRAYER FOR TODAY

Lord, You know my heart and its desire to be a positive influence in the world, to be able to provide exactly what people need when they need it. You also know my heart and its tendency to be deceitful and self-serving. Please give me strength to repent when I fail, and help me to become well trained in Your kingdom. In Jesus' name, Amen!

☀ TODAY'S TOPIC

Virtually all relationships come down to one-on-one dynamics. Individuals are, after all, individuals. When you have a relationship with a couple, it is ultimately a relationship with two individuals, since they each have their own mind, personality, experience, perspective, etc. This is part of the reason you can't expect to be an effective leader of a team if you haven't learned to lead one-on-one.

Jesus, as the leader of His team of twelve, had to develop them through the same transformational leadership cycle, beginning with self-leadership. Then in Matthew 10:5-10, we see Him sending them out in teams of two. This accomplished several purposes, one of which was to further their development in one-on-one leadership in preparation for the day when they would need to carry on without Him and lead effectively in a much larger context.

The rest of Chapter 10 is a lengthy set of instructions, encouragements and warnings — *whatever [they] needed, old or new, exactly when [they] needed it* (MATTHEW 13:52 MSG). He is modeling exactly what He wants them to become, **well-trained in God's kingdom**. He could do this because He had gone through the same process Himself. He didn't arrive on earth filled with power and ready to rule; He came as a vulnerable baby having to start from scratch.

It's very difficult to take people where you've never been, just as it's difficult to command trust if you are not giving it. Jesus lovingly led His team of twelve, stretching them with tender care and entrusting great authority to them — all the while knowing one would betray Him. He could do this because He knew the final victory was never in doubt. You can do it for the same reason

💼 LOOK INSIDE

Are you able to look at failures as your greatest learning opportunities and retain confidence that final victory is not in doubt? Think back through the greatest lessons you've learned. Haven't most of them come in times of painful testing? Do you see God's tender care in stretching and preserving you? What trials en route to becoming *well-trained in God's kingdom* would make your personal highlight reel?

_____

_____

_____

★ KEY CONCEPT

Leading team and family is merely an extension of the training you've already been through in self-leadership and one-on-one leadership. It's about building trust and serving together in a mission that exceeds yourself.

♀ A POINT TO PONDER

Family leadership is the ultimate in life-role leadership. Although it may lack the perks that can be easily seen and counted by the financial world, it is durable, with implications far beyond your lifetime. Never shortchange its importance.

✈ NEXT STEPS

Team/Family leadership frequently pits vocation against family. Each demands and seems to deserve more time than you can give it. The choices you make during this time reveal a lot about your true values, including the degree to which you are **driven versus called**. (Note: See *The HEART of a Great Leader Study Guide* for more information on driven versus called.)

The CEO of a well-known financial firm, after suffering two divorces, concluded that he had "a wife-selection problem." He went to a counselor who gave him a different assessment: "The good news is you do not have a wife-selection problem; the bad news is you have a husband-behavior problem." Fortunately, he listened. And changed.

How are you handling the choices? What changes might you need to make?

_____

_____

_____

_____

_____

_____

_____

ORGANIZATIONAL/COMMUNITY LEADERSHIP

QUOTE FOR TODAY

By valuing relationships and results, Jesus created the environment for developing an effective organization.

KEN BLANCHARD AND PHIL HODGES

WHAT GOD'S WORD SAYS

I will build my church, and the gates of Hades will not overcome it.
MATTHEW 16:18

Then Jesus came to them and said, All authority in heaven and on earth has been given to me. Therefore go and make disciples of all nations, baptizing them in the name of the Father and of the Son and of the Holy Spirit, and teaching them to obey everything I have commanded you. And surely I am with you always, to the very end of the age.
MATTHEW 28:18-20

PAUSE AND REFLECT

Consider the implications of Jesus' words in these verses from Matthew. *All authority in heaven and on earth has been given to me ... And surely I am with you always.* Is it any wonder why we say that Jesus is the only perfect leadership role model? *Let us fix our eyes on Jesus, the author and perfecter of our faith, who for the joy set before him endured the cross, scorning its shame, and sat down at the right hand of the throne of God* (HEBREWS 12:2).

This short lifetime, this opportunity you have right now to lead, is your one and only opportunity to follow Jesus' pattern of faithfulness to the mission given Him by the Father. It cost Him His life, but note that it ended with the Father giving Him all authority and seating Him on a throne at His right hand. What are you willing to endure *for the joy set before you*?

A PRAYER FOR TODAY

Lord, thank You for patiently growing me and preparing me for community leadership. Thank You for Jesus' promise to be with me always. Help me to fix my eyes on Him and remain faithful to the mission You have given me. In Jesus' name, Amen!

TODAY'S TOPIC

Community leadership is not restricted or defined by a formal position. It is the willingness to speak out for your values in a manner that recognizes the rights of others and the obligation to honor God in all you do.

The consequences of community leadership may come as a test of conviction when challenged or attacked. They may come as a temptation to compromise principle for practicality. They may come as a temptation in the form of recognition that tempts pride. They call for the leader to answer the questions **"Who am I?"** and **"Whose am I?"** again and again and again.

We urge you not to take your life-role leadership and relationships for granted, relying too much on their resilience and your ability to regain lost ground, lost intimacy, and lost love. Marriage and family are far too precious — gifts directly from the hand of God.

Another mistake many leaders today make is spending most of their time and energy trying to improve things at the organizational level before ensuring that they have adequately addressed their own credibility at individual, one-on-one, or team leadership levels.

LOOK INSIDE

Why do you desire to lead at the organizational/community level? Understanding that your motivation in the future may be purer than it is now, try to be really honest with yourself about what appeals to you now. Rank these in current motivational appeal with 1 being the highest.

__ The challenge
__ Financial reward
__ Prestige
__ Desire to develop others
__ Security

__ Prove that I am worthwhile
__ Accomplish something important
__ See if I have what it takes
__ Obey God's calling for me

__ Be a model leader
__ Have influential friends
__ Fulfill the Great Commission
__ Make my family proud

★ KEY CONCEPT

Organizational and community leadership are high-demand roles. The problems you face are more complex, the consequences are greater, the temptations may be more subtle but no less intense, and your "enemies" are likely to increase. Your commitment to lead like Jesus even when it feels like you are risking everything must be rock solid

♀ A POINT TO PONDER

Jesus replied, "No one who puts his hand to the plow and looks back is fit for service in the kingdom of God (LUKE 9:62). What would be most likely to tempt you to look back?

_____

_____

_____

◁ NEXT STEPS

As you meditate in prayer, asking God to search your heart and reveal His concerns for you, from what do you need to repent?

_____

_____

What areas of weakness do you need to strengthen?

_____

_____

What vulnerabilities or natural blind spots are you aware of that need support from trusted friends to protect you from failing under pressure?

_____

_____

WEEK THREE
DEVELOP YOUR VISION

MEMORY VERSE FOR THE WEEK

"For I know the plans I have for you," declares the Lord, "plans to prosper you and not to harm you, plans to give you hope and a future."
JEREMIAH 29:11

The visionary role — setting the course and the destination of your family, team, or organization — is your domain as the leader. This doesn't mean you do it in a vacuum, but after getting whatever counsel you need, it remains one of your primary responsibilities.

According to Ken and Jesse Stoner in their book, *Full Steam Ahead: The Power of Vision*, a compelling vision has three parts.

1.   Your purpose. What "business" are you in? Where are you going and why? Or in terms of your family, what is your family all about? Where is your family going and why?

2.   Your picture of the future. What will your future look like if you are accomplishing your purpose?

3.   Your values. What do you stand for? On what principles will you make your ongoing decisions?

A compelling vision tells people who they are, where they are going, and what will guide their journey. This week's study sheds light on this important process as we look at the first two of these three parts of a compelling vision: your purpose and your picture of the future.

It should be very encouraging to you to memorize and meditate on the verse for this week, knowing that God already has a purpose and a picture of the future for you. If that isn't enough to light your jets, couple it with this truth from ROMANS 8:37-39. *In all these things we are more than conquerors through him who loved us. For I am convinced that neither death nor life, neither angels nor demons, neither the present nor the future, nor any powers, neither height nor depth, nor anything else in all creation, will be able to separate us from the love of God that is in Christ Jesus our Lord.*

DEVELOP YOUR VISION
TWO ROLES OF SERVANT LEADERSHIP

QUOTE FOR TODAY

The essence of leadership is to see and to serve — to envision and equip.
STEVE GARDNER

WHAT GOD'S WORD SAYS

Moses said to the Lord, "May the Lord, the God of the spirits of all mankind, appoint a man over this community to go out and come in before them, one who will lead them out and bring them in, so the Lord's people will not be like sheep without a shepherd."
NUMBERS 27:15-17

PAUSE AND REFLECT

In the passage above, Moses is asking God to provide a successor who will perform two functions: *lead them out* and *bring them in*. How might *lead them out* equate with casting a vision?

_____

_____

_____

_____

How might *bring them in* equate with implementing the vision to its fulfillment?

_____

_____

_____

_____

A PRAYER FOR TODAY

Lord, I want to be a complete leader. I want to provide direction and I want to make sure implementation happens so that we reach our destination. Please give me the wisdom I need to do both. In Jesus' name, Amen!

☀ TODAY'S TOPIC

Skeptics of servant leadership contend that the words *servant* and *leader* don't go together. How can you lead and serve? People who think that way don't understand that there are two parts to the servant leadership that Jesus exemplified:

1. A visionary role — setting the course and the destination (**deciding the right things to do**)

2. An implementation role — doing things right with a focus on serving

Some people think leadership is about vision while management is about implementation, but leaders are responsible (and held accountable) for both. We consider both roles as servant leadership roles.

In Numbers 27:18-21, God granted Moses' request by providing Joshua. Then He gave two specific commands that, if followed, would give Joshua what he would need to fulfill both roles of leadership.

1. *He is to stand before Eleazar the priest, who will obtain decisions for him by inquiring of the Urim before the Lord* (NUMBERS 27:21). This is direction — providing the vision Joshua would need to **lead them out**.

2. *Give him some of your authority so the whole Israelite community will obey him* (NUMBERS 27:20). This is implementation — providing the authority Joshua would need to serve a rebellious people and **bring them in** to the Promised Land.

In the New Testament, Jesus consistently modeled the visionary and implementation roles. Both by word and deed, He cast a vision of the kingdom of heaven that was completely contrary to that of the religious establishment. And He simultaneously served in implementation by concentrating His effort on the training of twelve ordinary men who would need to do extraordinary things.

💼 LOOK INSIDE

How well do you think you fulfill the two roles of leadership for those within your influence? Are you providing a compelling vision?

Not compelling - Very compelling

1   2   3   4   5

Are you serving your team in the implementation of the vision?

Not actively - - - - - - - - - - - - - - - - - - - Very actively

1   2   3   4   5

Explain any difference between the way you respond to positive and negative feedback.

_____

_____

_____

_____

★ KEY CONCEPT

Vision and implementation are two sides of the same coin — each equally important. We lead by setting course and direction; we serve by empowering and supporting others in implementation.

💡 A POINT TO PONDER

Inspirational leaders are usually visionaries with great ideas and persuasive conviction. It's not unusual, however, for them to lack some of the organizational and detail skills needed to refine all the tactics called for in the grand strategic plan. This doesn't relieve them of those responsibilities; it just demonstrates their need for a team. For them to be successful, they need to make their team successful. This is the essence of serving them.

Leaders who are strong implementers may need help with vision and inspiration. This can be difficult to admit, but it's not impossible to overcome. Wise counsel from gifted team members as well as people outside of the organization can increase a leader's ability to develop and communicate a compelling vision. Just as God provided Eleazar for Joshua, He can provide someone for you if you have this need.

NEXT STEPS

Based on your self-assessment in the "Look Inside" section on page 45, what role of leadership creates the biggest challenge for you? What will you do about it?

_____

_____

_____

_____

_____

_____

_____

_____

_____

DEVELOP YOUR VISION
PERSONAL VISION — PURPOSE

" QUOTE FOR TODAY

True happiness is not attained through self-gratification but through fidelity to a worthy purpose.
HELEN KELLER

WHAT GOD'S WORD SAYS

Many are the plans in a man's heart, but it is the Lord's purpose that prevails.
PROVERBS 19:21

Trust in the Lord with all your heart and lean not on your own understanding; in all your ways acknowledge him, and he will make your paths straight.
PROVERBS 3:5-6

❚❚ PAUSE AND REFLECT

Many people expect to live 70 years or so in a world filled with challenges and uncertainty — and then cease to exist. Followers of Jesus have a different perspective on life. As recipients of God's grace and eternal life, they have become His ambassadors in the ministry of reconciliation. How do you think this might affect their view of purpose? How would you express yours?

_____

_____

_____

🙏 A PRAYER FOR TODAY

Lord, thank You for taking my guilt and exchanging it for the righteousness of Jesus. Thank You for adopting me into Your family and giving me an eternal purpose. Please lift my vision to Your purpose that prevails and help me to trust in You with all my heart. In Jesus' name, Amen!

☀ TODAY'S TOPIC

Before seeking to influence the thinking and behavior of others, it is important to have a sense of your own personal vision. Who are you? What is your purpose? Where are you going? How do you picture the future for yourself? What will guide your journey? What are your personal values?

A purpose/mission statement tells you who you are and identifies your purpose on earth. Richard Bolles, in his best-selling book *What Color Is Your Parachute?*, suggests that there are three parts to writing a personal mission statement. The first two are goals that every person should pursue, while the third is individually unique.

The first part of any mission statement is becoming more aware of what God is doing and wants to do in your life.

The second part of a personal mission statement is to identify the impact your life will have on the world. If you ask people whether they want to make the world a better place, they all say yes. But when you ask them how they plan to make the world a better place, they stare blankly as if you're speaking a foreign language. The way to make the world a better place is through your moment-to-moment activities. Every day is full of opportunities to make the world a better place as you interact with people.

The third and final aspect of a mission statement is unique to you. What work activities so capture your interest that you lose track of time? That probably is why you are here on earth. The Lord did not put you here to fight against yourself; He put you together with a unique set of gifts and abilities so that people can see Him through the things you do.

💼 LOOK INSIDE

"Your purpose is what kind of business you are in as a person."
KEN BLANCHARD AND NORMAN VINCENT PEALE

How clear are you about your personal mission? If you are a person of wide interests, you may have an interesting life that lacks focus — a mile wide and an inch deep. Effective leaders recognize the need to push some interests into the background to focus more closely on their unique passions. Take a few minutes to list your interests. Then force yourself to narrow them into a much smaller list that you are truly passionate about. Does your time budget reflect the focus you want?

My Interests	My Passions
_____	_____
_____	_____
_____	_____
_____	_____

★ KEY CONCEPT

God did not design you to wander purposelessly in the hope that something good would happen to you — something good enough to make life's trials tolerable. He has both a purpose and a plan for you. Are you willing to search for it?

💡 A POINT TO PONDER

To lead like Jesus means to operate with the mind of Christ. How did He view people? Did He treat them as objects to be used, a means to gain power or wealth? That would have been yielding to Satan's temptation — as do many human leaders. Instead, Jesus treated lost humanity — *enemies of God* — with love and compassion, choosing to sacrifice His own life for their redemption.

✈ NEXT STEPS

As a start to writing (or revising) your personal mission statement, focus on the three parts presented in Today's Topic.

1. What is God doing? How do you see Him at work in the world? What events has He allowed in your life that have motivated you to reach out to others? What needs do you desire to fill?

    _____

    _____

    _____

    _____

2. What kinds of daily activities (nothing heroic) do you do with the attitude of being a blessing? Jesus' suggestion that giving a cup of water in His name merited a reward lets us know that even simple acts of kindness count.

    _____

    _____

    _____

3. What gifts (special abilities) do you have? What do you love to do? What are you passionate about? These are not accidents; they relate to God's design for you and your purpose.

    _____

    _____

    _____

    _____

DEVELOP YOUR VISION
PERSONAL VISION — PICTURE OF THE FUTURE

〝 QUOTE FOR TODAY

The real voyage of discovery consists not in seeking new landscapes but in having new eyes.
MARCEL PROUST

WHAT GOD'S WORD SAYS

I pray also that the eyes of your heart may be enlightened in order that you may know the hope to which he has called you, the riches of his glorious inheritance in the saints.
EPHESIANS 1:18

The most important thing is that I complete my mission, the work that the Lord Jesus gave me
ACTS 20:24 (NCV)

‖ PAUSE AND REFLECT

Think about the **eyes of your heart**. What do you treasure enough that you are constantly searching for it? What would the answer be if the **eyes of your heart** were like the eyes of Jesus' heart?

What do you think? If a man owns a hundred sheep, and one of them wanders away, will he not leave the ninety-nine on the hills and go to look for the one that wandered off? And if he finds it, I tell you the truth, he is happier about that one sheep than about the ninety-nine that did not wander off. In the same way your Father in heaven is not willing that any of these little ones should be lost.
MATTHEW 18:12-14

People are vulnerable. How did Jesus care for them? How will you?

_____

_____

_____

🙏 A PRAYER FOR TODAY

Lord, thank You for Paul's prayer in Ephesians 1:18. Please enlighten the eyes of my heart. Give me a glimpse of Your perspective and help me to aim higher than I ever thought possible. Draw me to Your glory so that I don't make my vision all about me, and give me Your relentless compassion for vulnerable people. In Jesus' name, Amen!

☀ TODAY'S TOPIC

Reread today's Quote of the Day: "The real voyage of discovery consists not in seeking new landscapes but in having new eyes." One way it could be interpreted is to stop falling for "The grass is greener ..." syndrome. A change in landscape (a different state, a different job, a different car, a different church, a different spouse) — these are not the answer to your needs.

It's easy to look at an established leader and think I could do that if I had his start; conveniently forgetting, of course, that he didn't have his start when he started. He had the same dilemma you have: figuring out what he was designed to do and applying himself to it.

Most of those who score high on the test of life have a special crutch, a crib sheet. It's a snapshot of their view of success. It informs them by reminding them of what the goal looks like. It motivates them by reminding them that the cost is worth it.

It's just a simple snapshot, but it can speak volumes to you because of its vast hidden rewards — things not yet seen except through the eyes of your heart. Think of it as a Polaroid that is not quite done developing: it looks good now, but the most beautiful details are yet to appear. And some of those are today's painful memories that will be transformed into trophies of God's grace — stepping stones to significant service.

💼 LOOK INSIDE

How do you define significance? Is it money and prestige? Or have you already experienced their inability to satisfy? Look at today's verses. Ephesians 1:18 gives a countercultural snapshot of riches. And Acts 20:24 gives us a glimpse into Paul's idea of an epitaph as he is departing Ephesus.

Then notice how the Ephesian elders feel about Paul. *They all wept as they embraced him and kissed him. What grieved them most was his statement that they would never see his face again. Then they accompanied him to the ship* (ACTS 20:37-38).

Paul faced all kinds of hardships but was sustained by the power of his vision. What kind of epitaph would inspire you to persevere through challenging times?

_____

_____

_____

★ KEY CONCEPT

Carrying a snapshot of your preferred future based on your purpose is one of the most important elements in fulfilling your destiny — God's plan for you.

♀ A POINT TO PONDER

Vision is the fundamental force that drives everything else in our lives. It impassions us with a sense of the unique contribution that's ours to make.
STEPHEN COVEY

⏎ NEXT STEPS

Take your purpose thoughts from yesterday and your significance thoughts from today. Begin describing your personal snapshot.

_____

_____

_____

_____

_____

_____

_____

_____

_____

ORGANIZATIONAL VISION — PURPOSE

99 QUOTE FOR TODAY

Nothing is as necessary for success as the single-minded pursuit of an objective.
FRED SMITH

WHAT GOD'S WORD SAYS

In the same way that you gave me a mission in the world, I give them a mission in the world.
JOHN 17:18 (MSG)

[Mission] To prepare God's people for works of service, so that the body of Christ may be built up [Vision] until we all reach unity in the faith and in the knowledge of the Son of God and become mature, attaining to the whole measure of the fullness of Christ.
EPHESIANS 4:12-13

PAUSE AND REFLECT

If all of this talk about vision and purpose produces stress in you, consider this: Victor Frankl advises that "mental health is based on a certain degree of mental tension, the tension between what one has already achieved and what one still ought to accomplish ... the gap between what one is and what one should become."

The same gap exists in an organization. It will never become what it should become if no one knows what that is. Accept the tension — the positive stress — of discovering and determining your organization's concrete assignment. It naturally grows out of your personal vision and purpose.

A PRAYER FOR TODAY

Lord, thank You for giving Jesus a mission in the world. And thank You that He has given us one as well. Help me to understand our vision and mission and to communicate them clearly as I lead those You have placed within my influence. Thank You for the significance Your mission brings into our daily lives. In Jesus' name, Amen!

TODAY'S TOPIC

Leadership is about going somewhere. It is especially important to have a compelling vision that provides direction and focuses everyone's energy on getting where they are headed. To engage the hearts and minds of others, you must be able to communicate your purpose, your picture of the future, and your values. Today, we look at purpose, reflected in a mission statement.

What business are you in? What are you trying to accomplish? An effective mission statement should express a higher purpose for the greater good that gives meaning to the efforts of each individual involved in your organization. It should motivate people as it sets the direction for where you are going.

Unclear direction inevitably leads to misalignment and a host of related problems. Ken's father offered this chilling statement as part of his answer to why he retired early from the peacetime Navy: "Since nobody knows what we are supposed to be doing, too many leaders think their full time job is making other people feel unimportant." That's tragic. Especially because it's preventable.

LOOK INSIDE

If the people in your organization are not excited about your mission statement, they will lose both alignment and direction, become self-focused, and lose their way. Your responsibility as a leader includes this part of strategic planning.

★ KEY CONCEPT

Your organization needs an effective mission statement that gives meaning to the efforts of each team member. It should be short, memorable and motivational.

A POINT TO PONDER

One church expresses their mission this way: "Our mission is to make Jesus smile." If you are leading a business, you will want something connected more closely to the nature of the business, but the thought is still inspiring. How can you state your purpose in a way that would make Jesus smile?

_____

_____

_____

NEXT STEPS

Begin writing (or revising) an organizational mission statement based on what you have discovered in this session. Keep in mind that it's more about how you think than what you think. Writing your vision forces you to move away from micromanagement toward macro-leadership.

Don't worry about crafting the perfect statement that you will live with for the rest of your life; any statement like that would be so vague it could pass for every organization's statement. For now, just take a stab at a first draft, knowing that you will refine it in the process of this study.

Jot some initial thoughts regarding a mission statement for your organization.

_____

_____

_____

A vision, or view of the future, is an ongoing, evolving, hopeful look into the future that stirs the hearts and minds of people who know they will never see its end or limit. Begin to imagine what your organization (and the part of the world you influence) will look like if you succeed in your mission.

- What problems will you have solved?

_____

_____

- How will people benefit?

_____

_____

- How will God be glorified?

_____

_____

- What will your organization and its people have become in the process?

_____

_____

DEVELOP YOUR VISION
BRINGING IT ALL HOME

99 QUOTE FOR TODAY

Whatever form our most pressing problems may take — ultimately, all are related to the disintegration of the family.

GEORGE H. W. BUSH

WHAT GOD'S WORD SAYS

Even while these people were worshiping the Lord, they were serving their idols. To this day their children and grandchildren continue to do as their fathers did.

2 KINGS 17:41

Fathers, do not exasperate your children; instead, bring them up in the training and instruction of the Lord.

EPHESIANS 6:4

❚❚ PAUSE AND REFLECT

Can you recall times as a child when you saw something your parents did, and you said to yourself, "I'll never do that?" And now, as a parent, you discover yourself doing it? Sometimes it's good for a laugh. Sometimes, it's tragic.

The point is that values are more about what we live than what we say. And values are **always** transmitted to our children. Did you notice it in the 2 Kings passage? Parents talked about God but served their idols. And their children did the same. Why not? The walk is always more real than the talk.

What are your idols? Is your desire to excel at work really about the welfare of your family, or has it run slightly off the tracks? Take a few moments to consider what you're trying to prove. Who is your audience?

🙏 A PRAYER FOR TODAY

Lord, thank You for the unique way You've wired me. Thank You for my desire to change things and to make a difference. Please help me to keep it healthy — to not let it become an idol that takes my devotion and robs You and my family. Help me to keep my priorities straight. In Jesus' name, Amen!

☀ TODAY'S TOPIC

It's time to meddle. As a motivated leader (Is there any other kind?), you are likely to be focused on running your business, organization, or team as effectively as possible. No problem. Unless that focus becomes your primary commitment; then it's a big problem. Could it happen without your realizing it?

> "Ask the average person which is more important to him, making money or being devoted to his family, and virtually everyone will answer family without hesitation. But watch how the average person actually lives out his life. See where he really invests his time and energy, and he will give away the fact that he does not really live by what he says he believes. He has let himself be persuaded that if he leaves for work earlier in the morning and comes home more tired at night, he is proving how devoted he is to his family by expending himself to provide them all the things they have seen advertised."
> HAROLD KUSHNER

Regardless of your role at work and the extent of its demands, your leadership at home is a primary calling and commitment. Work exists to support it, not the other way around.

Judge Leon Yankwich said in 1928 that there are no illegitimate children — only illegitimate parents. Although our technology has come a long way since 1928, we have not yet invented a remote control capable of discerning and providing for our children's greatest need. Only self-deception would allow us to believe we can run our home on autopilot and avoid child neglect.

Make sure to apply at home what you are learning about vision and purpose. Your children will inevitably follow someone. Whose influence will fill the leadership vacuum you leave if you don't step up?

💼 LOOK INSIDE

Do some honest detective work to find evidence of your priorities. Ask for input from your family.

Evidence that I could be neglecting
my leadership at work:

_____

_____

_____

Evidence that I could be neglecting
my leadership at home:

_____

_____

_____

Evidence that I could be neglecting
my leadership at work:

_____

_____

_____

_____

_____

_____

_____

_____

Evidence that I could be neglecting
my leadership at home:

_____

_____

_____

_____

_____

_____

_____

_____

★ KEY CONCEPT

Your family has the same need for a clear vision and purpose as your business or organization.
Lead them in developing it.

💡 A POINT TO PONDER

Your Name

You got it from your father; it was all he had to give
So it's yours to use and cherish as long as you may live.
If you lose the watch he gave you, it can always be replaced
But a black mark on your name, son, can never be erased.
It was clean the day you took it, and a worthy name to bear
When he got it from his father, there was no dishonor there.
So make sure you guard it wisely; after all is said and done
You'll be glad the name is spotless when you give it to your son.

— AS TOLD TO LOU HOLTZ

◢ NEXT STEPS

Suppose you were to ask your spouse and children (or grandchildren): What are the most important things about our family, our top three values? How do you think they would answer?

_____

_____

_____

_____

_____

_____

_____

_____

_____

After you've imagined their response, go ask them. For real. Talk about it. It doesn't need to be a long discussion. Tell them it's important to you and that you'd like them to think about it and discuss it again later. Allow this to help you build a deliberate family identity — something as unique and important to you as your name.

WEEK FOUR
VALUES, GOALS, AND IMPLEMENTATION

MEMORY VERSE FOR THE WEEK

Your attitude should be the same as that of Christ Jesus.
PHILIPPIANS 2:5

In previous sessions we've explored the first two of three elements in a compelling vision: your purpose and your picture of the future. This week we move to the third: your values. First,

Everyone is responsible for identifying personal values and setting priorities accordingly. Then, if you are leading at the organizational level, you need to define your organization's values as well. Governing how you behave in your organization, your values are the nonnegotiable principles that define your character as a leader. They should be influenced by and grow out of your personal values.

Always remember that leading like Jesus means leading with the mind of Christ. *Do nothing out of selfish ambition or vain conceit, but in humility consider others better than yourselves. Each of you should look not only to your own interests, but also to the interests of others. Your attitude should be the same as that of Christ Jesus.*
PHILIPPIANS 2:3-5

Jesus viewed people as objects — objects of God's affection. And He treated them that way. Recognizing their vulnerability, He reached out to the disenfranchised in a way they could feel and appreciate. He healed them, He taught them, He hung out with them, He protected them.

Why else would He step between a self-righteous mob and a woman caught in adultery? His values of forgiveness and reconciliation trumped the values of justice and punishment. He took radical action to show the religious establishment the bankruptcy of their self-serving values.

We pray that the final week in this study will assist you in completing some very important work — both personal and corporate — in setting a direction that will help you shine like stars in the universe (Philippians 2:15).

VALUES, GOALS, AND IMPLEMENTATION
VALUES DIFFERENTIATE

99 QUOTE FOR TODAY

True success in servant leadership depends on how clearly the values are defined, ordered, and lived by the leader.

KEN BLANCHARD AND PHIL HODGES

WHAT GOD'S WORD SAYS

I know, my God, that you test the heart and are pleased with integrity ...
1 CHRONICLES 29:17

Then the Lord said to Satan, "Have you considered my servant Job? There is no one on earth like him; he is blameless and upright, a man who fears God and shuns evil. And he still maintains his integrity, though you incited me against him to ruin him without any reason."
JOB 2:3

❚❚ PAUSE AND REFLECT

How important do you really think your values are? How about your organization's values? Has it occurred to you that your organization's values — if carefully chosen and lived out — could play a major role in differentiating you from your competition? Organizations that give lip service to strong values are a dime a dozen, but when the values rule behavior, people notice.

Think of some common character complaints associated with your industry. What might happen if you confronted them head on with a value you promoted **and** exemplified?

A PRAYER FOR TODAY

Lord, thank You for rewarding integrity. Please give me wisdom as I wrestle with what values to emphasize. And help me develop the integrity and courage to live them. I want to be like Job in trusting You in spite of circumstances. In Jesus' name, Amen!

☀ **TODAY'S TOPIC**

For good or ill, your values set you apart. Remember the slogan, "Image is everything?" It was a clever play on words for a camera manufacturer, but the implied value was — and is — bankrupt. And in spite of the millions spent on it, thinking people never accepted it.

How about this one? "What happens in Vegas stays in Vegas." This "Sin City" slogan touches on much more than gambling. What insidious values does it imply?

- Your sins will not find you out.

- What is hidden isn't real or doesn't matter.

- Betrayal isn't real unless you let it out of containment and expose it.

- Don't worry about conscience; it wants to limit you, not protect you.

- You don't have to take the consequences home.

What consequences do you ever not take with you? No one can outrun the consequences of ungodly behavior. But something does "stay in Vegas": your money.

Contrast those negative values with the one promoted by Frank Wylie, former director of public relations for Chrysler.

> Tell the truth because it is the smartest thing to do, and people will begin to believe you. Keep telling the truth, all of it, and people will believe you. Some will say that you can't tell the whole truth. That's hogwash. If two people know something, it's public, and all of it will be told sooner or later. Tell it all, and you surprise and make believers out of people.
>
> Honesty is so rare it's perhaps the most effective weapon available. Tell it all, and tell it first, and you get the best shot at the world. Hold it back, any of it, and you'll be playing catch-up; you'll never really make it.

It could be stated this way: Dare to always tell the whole truth.

LOOK INSIDE

What values do you want to differentiate you and your organization? What can you hold up with long-term confidence and strive to live up to?

_____

_____

_____

KEY CONCEPT

Godly values, spoken **and** lived, are a powerful ally that will set you apart over the long haul.

A POINT TO PONDER

Your personal values and your organizational values may not be identical because they relate to different domains. But they should be in harmony. If they are in conflict, you will inevitably find yourself in situations where you must compromise one for another. Do everything in your power to change or modify organizational values that conflict with personal values that are nonnegotiable.

NEXT STEPS

Begin thinking about the values you want to characterize your life and your organization. Take to heart The Quote of the Day: "True success in servant leadership depends on how clearly the values are defined, ordered, and lived by the leader."

_____

_____

_____

_____

_____

99 QUOTE FOR TODAY

Clarifying your values is the essential first step toward a richer, fuller, more productive life.
CARL ROGERS

WHAT GOD'S WORD SAYS

... I will put my laws in their minds and write them on their hearts. I will be their God, and they will be my people.
HEBREWS 8:10

Let those who love the Lord hate evil, for he guards the lives of his faithful ones and delivers them from the hand of the wicked.
PSALM 97:10

PAUSE AND REFLECT

Consider this line that appeared in the *California Tribune:* "There are so many men who can figure costs, and so few who can measure values."

How are you at measuring? Have you identified clear values or do you shoot from the hip?

I live by feel --I live by clear values

1   2   3   4   5

Skill in measuring values requires discernment, and no one is born with it. It usually follows a lot of experience, careful consideration, close attention to God's Word and the prompting of His Spirit. What is the source of your values?

_____

_____

_____

A PRAYER FOR TODAY

Lord, You have promised to write Your laws in my mind and on my heart. Thank You for Your revelation of truth. Help me to recognize that any difference between Your values and mine are proof of my imperfect perspective. Help me to value what You value, to love what You love and hate what You hate. In Jesus' name, Amen!

☼ TODAY'S TOPIC

Values govern how you behave in your organization. They are the nonnegotiable principles that define character in a leader.

Values are both descriptive and prescriptive. First, they describe the qualities that are most important to you. They may or may not fully align with the values that are currently most evident in your life, but they should fully align with the values you desire to be most evident. To the extent they resemble what is currently most evident, they are descriptive. To the extent they resemble what you want, they are prescriptive — both for you and for everyone else in the organization.

Unfortunately, fewer than 10 percent of the organizations around the world have clear, written values. Of the ones that do, most have a list that is either not rank ordered or too long to be effective — or both. Research shows that if you really want to impact behavior, you can't emphasize more than three or four values, because people can't focus on more.

And focus is a key word. Life is about value conflicts, and when these conflicts arise, people need to know what values they should focus on — which values trump others. Without guidelines, people will create their own order of priority. Once this happens, you lose alignment and momentum. Energy that goes in competing directions is worse than merely wasted.

Jesus took a list of 683 laws and boiled them down to two rank-ordered values:

1. Love God with all your heart, soul, and mind.
2. Love your neighbor as yourself.

It's hard to match the simple, comprehensive elegance of those values, but you can at least copy the principle. Settle on two or three — no more than four — that will trump the rest when push comes to shove. Make sure you really believe them and are willing to force yourself and your organization to live by them.

💼 LOOK INSIDE

Look again at the second verse for today: *Let those who love the Lord hate evil, for he guards the lives of his faithful ones and delivers them from the hand of the wicked* (PSALM 97:10). This raises some interesting questions. Do you hate evil? Or have you declared a truce with some sector of evil? Perhaps one you haven't recognized as being all that damaging ... yet. Has God written His laws (values) on your heart? Where do you see some divergence between His and yours?

_____

_____

_____

⭐ KEY CONCEPT

Godly values, spoken and lived, are a powerful ally that will set you apart over the long haul.

💡 A POINT TO PONDER

Our value is the sum of our values.
JOE BATTEN

✈ NEXT STEPS

Compare any two words at a time as you consider this sample list of words with value implications. Eliminate the less desirable until you have only four left (including any you might add to the list). Mull over your final four for use in tomorrow's session

Faith	Growth	Passion	Balance
Wisdom	Honesty	Courage	Knowledge
Integrity	Efficiency	Fun	Service
Achievement	Commitment	Perfection	Teamwork
Effectiveness	Trust	Independence	Status
Creativity	Loyalty	Fairness	Money
Competence	Fitness	Quality	Family

VALUES, GOALS, AND IMPLEMENTATION
YOUR VALUES AS BEHAVIORS

QUOTE FOR TODAY

There can be no happiness if the things we believe in are different from the things we do.
DR. ROBERT CONROY

WHAT GOD'S WORD SAYS

Knowing the correct password — saying "Master, Master," for instance — isn't going to get you anywhere with me. What is required is serious obedience — doing what my Father wills.
MATTHEW 7:21 (MSG)

For the eyes of the Lord range throughout the earth to strengthen those whose hearts are fully committed to him ...
2 CHRONICLES 16:9

PAUSE AND REFLECT

Anyone, if required, can create an impressive list of values. Our God-given conscience intuitively knows the difference between good and bad. The question is whether our list bears any resemblance to our life — whether our professed values have found a home in our head and our heart. Your calendar and your wallet make powerful statements about the values that really occupy your head and heart. What do they say about yours?

_____

_____

_____

_____

A PRAYER FOR TODAY

Lord, it doesn't always feel like You're paying attention, but I thank You for watching to strengthen those whose hearts are fully committed to You. I want that to be true of me. Help me to adopt Your values and to put them into practice daily. In Jesus' name, Amen!

☀ TODAY'S TOPIC

A statement by Sigmund Freud gives insight into values: "Faith is much better than belief. Belief is when someone else does the thinking." I'd like to take it one step further: Until your values become your behavior, they're really someone else's values you're trying on for size.

Values are only platitudes until they are proven on the battlefield of your life. When you have to sacrifice something precious to honor something even more precious, you reveal your core values.

Discovering your core values is not a simple exercise in brainstorming noble words and selecting the ones that sound the most impressive. It is a search for what you believe are the most important, enduring qualities in life — ones for which you will give up everything else if necessary.

In Matthew 13:45-46, Jesus compares the kingdom of heaven with a pearl of great value. Think of yourself as the merchant He describes when He says, ***"When he found one of great value, he went away and sold everything he had and bought it."*** Think of the implications: this pearl cost the merchant **everything he had!** But did the merchant complain? No, it was his choice. The pearl was worth it.

Your life — your behavior — proves what is worth it to you. Think carefully about what your true values should be. And even more carefully about what they are. What is your battlefield revealing?

💼 LOOK INSIDE

Think again about the words you chose in the last session. Have you arrived at a list of four or less? Are they pearls of great value to you? Is there one on the list you would surrender in favor of something not on the list?

As time goes on, you are likely to discover a "yes" to the last question. If you remain conscious of your values as you experience life, you will be constantly evaluating, testing, discerning what is worth everything you have. And you may discover that you need to re-prioritize. As long as your choice is in obedience to God's Spirit rather than a compromise with your lower nature, you'll be making a good trade.

★ KEY CONCEPT

Core values translate into core behaviors. If the behaviors you want are not evident in the heat of battle, your professed values do not belong to you.

A POINT TO PONDER

When you need to change your behavior, uncover your deepest beliefs — the hidden commitments that compete with your stated values — and examine them for the flaws you have not previously discerned. Replace them with pearls of greater value

NEXT STEPS

Once you have settled on the three or four words that represent your pearls of greatest value at this point in your life, turn them into action statements. Follow Jesus' example and make them commands, short and to the point. Memorize them and allow them to help mold you into a more Jesus-like leader.

ACTION STATEMENTS
OPERATIONALLY DEFINED

QUOTE FOR TODAY

A magazine requested that J. Paul Getty submit a short article explaining his success. Here is what he sent. "Some people find oil. Others don't."

J. PAUL GETTY

WHAT GOD'S WORD SAYS

Do not merely listen to the word, and so deceive yourselves. Do what it says.

JAMES 1:22

Who is wise and understanding among you? Let him show it by his good life, by deeds done in the humility that comes from wisdom.

JAMES 3:13

PAUSE AND REFLECT

Do you think J. Paul Getty was just being silly and crediting luck for his success? Or was he really making a statement about action trumping wishful thinking?

Do you think James is likely to be impressed with a list of values? Or will he look for a list of deeds? Have you translated your values list into action statements yet? If so, are you taking action on your action statements? Describe.

_____

_____

_____

_____

A PRAYER FOR TODAY

Lord, I don't want to be self-deceived; I want to put truth into action. Help me discern what my values should look like in everyday life. In Jesus' name, Amen!

☼ TODAY'S TOPIC

Lead Like Jesus has organizational values that are ranked and worded as action statements. Let's take the first one as an example: "Glorify God in everything we do." Then we operationally define each one. For example, we will know that we are glorifying God in everything we do when we:

- Give God all the credit.

- Relinquish all problems to His care.

- Seek His face through worshiping together, studying together, and praying together.

- Love one another as He loves us by being a loving truth-teller, honoring each other's commitment, encouraging each other's health and well-being.

- Proceed boldly in living the gospel.

Although each bullet in this list may be driven by a belief and an attitude, each bullet can be readily seen in action. Are we relinquishing all problems to His care? Doing so does not make us passive spectators; we remain obediently active, but we repent of worry. Work and reliance on God make a perfect marriage. Adding worry turns the marriage into an unholy alliance and, yes, it is visible.

Defining our values operationally enables us to keep the values short and simple for easy memory while giving them enough substance to provide a basis for accountability. It also enables us to think through how they should look in our unique enterprise and culture.

It's possible that you could have the very same first value and define it operationally in an entirely different way. Because your enterprise and culture is unique, you will want to define the value in a way that makes the most impact in your world.

💼 LOOK INSIDE

How many times have you made New Year's resolutions that lasted for a month? Or a week? We've all been there. We need accountability to help us do the things we know we should.

Can you identify with Paul when he says, " ... *I have the desire to do what is good, but I cannot carry it out*" (ROMANS 7:18)? Sometimes your values put you in that position. Can you see how having them written as action statements that are operationally defined will help keep your feet to the fire? As unpleasant as that may sound, it can be very liberating because of the positive boundaries it provides. Jot a few thoughts about how you have found positive boundaries to be liberating in the past.

_____

_____

_____

★ KEY CONCEPT

Keep your list of values short and simple for easy memory, but define them sufficiently to provide a basis for accountability.

○ A POINT TO PONDER

The difficulty, my friends, is not to avoid death but to avoid unrighteousness.
SOCRATES

Should your clearly stated values help you avoid unrighteousness? What can you do to increase the likelihood?

_____

_____

_____

◁ NEXT STEPS

Take your value actions statements — your commands from yesterday's "Next Steps" — and begin defining them operationally.

_____

_____

_____

_____

_____

VALUES, GOALS, AND IMPLEMENTATION
IMPLEMENTING YOUR VISION AND GOALS

99 QUOTE FOR TODAY

Once your vision is set, you can establish goals to answer the question: what do you want people to focus on now?

KEN BLANCHARD AND PHIL HODGES

📖 WHAT GOD'S WORD SAYS

Whatever you do, work at it with all your heart, as working for the Lord, not for men, since you know that you will receive an inheritance from the Lord as a reward. It is the Lord Christ you are serving.

COLOSSIANS 3:23-24

❚❚ PAUSE AND REFLECT

Jack Paar was probably only half serious when he said, "Looking back, my life seems like one long obstacle race, with me as its chief obstacle." And yet we all have a sense that we are our own worst enemy — particularly when we fail to set goals that focus significant energy on the most important aspects of our life.

Contrast this thought with Paul's instruction to the Colossians. Use the space below on the left to list some goals you wish you had set ten years ago — goals that could have propelled you beyond your present level of development.

Use the space below on the right to list some goals that meet the standard of *work at it with all your heart, as working for the Lord.* Make them clear and measurable, and give them deadlines.

_____   _____

_____   _____

_____   _____

🙏 A PRAYER FOR TODAY

Lord, thank You for the reality that I serve You — even as I am serving my team in implementing our vision and mission. Please help me recognize the goals that will focus our energy on a day-to-day pursuit of the purpose You have given us. In Jesus' name, Amen

☀ TODAY'S TOPIC

The traditional pyramid hierarchy shows you as the leader at the top, responsible for providing the organizational vision — the picture of where you want to take the team and why. The team's role is to be responsive to your vision.

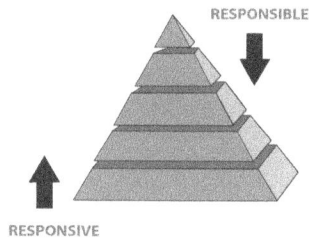

Once they have that picture, your leadership emphasis switches to the second role of leadership — implementation. You now become, in a sense, a servant of the vision, by serving the people you are asking to act according to the vision and accomplish the goals.

This requires you to take the traditional pyramid hierarchy and turn it upside down so the frontline people who are closest to your customers are at the top, where they can be responsible — able to respond — to them.

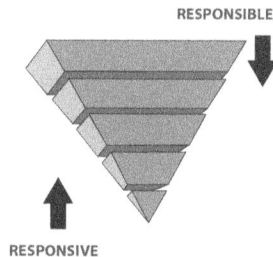

Now your role as the leader is to be responsive to your team's needs, training and developing them to deliver on the promises embedded in your vision, mission and values. Failure to do this is the reason many organizations get in trouble. All the energy moves away from the customers, up the hierarchy, because people feel they must please their bosses, leaving the customers neglected at the bottom of the hierarchy.

Jesus frequently clashed with the religious establishment because of their interest in protecting rules and regulations over the higher goal of love, forgiveness, and grace.

💼 LOOK INSIDE

How well are you serving your team in the implementation of all you are challenging them to accomplish? Are you being responsive to them so they can be responsible to your customers? Are you empowering them by providing the what, the how, and the why of excellent service? Do they have clear goals to keep them aligned and moving forward?

_____

_____

_____

⭐ KEY CONCEPT

Servant leadership is a continuous cycle of leading in vision and serving in implementation.

💡 A POINT TO PONDER

Every goal you set for your team should be accompanied by plans for what you can do to serve and empower them in their efforts.

✈ NEXT STEPS

Assess where you are currently in the two roles of leadership:

1. The visionary role — setting the course and the destination *(deciding the right things to do)*

2. The implementation role — *doing things right* with a focus on serving

Ask God for insight regarding ways to strengthen either of these. And ask for honest input from team members.

_____

_____

_____

AFTER WORDS

IN MAKING THE CLAIM THAT JESUS IS THE GREATEST LEADERSHIP ROLE MODEL OF ALL TIME WE HAVE IN ALL RESPECTS LIFTED HIM UP AS THE GREATEST FOLLOWER OF ALL TIME.

Leading like Jesus is a call to see our influence on the thinking, behavior and development of others as an extension and expression of our own followership. In this study of the Head, we have sought to provide insight into the process of abiding in the mind of Christ to guide the stewardship of our influence in the spirit of Romans 12:2.

> *Do not conform any longer to the (Leadership) patterns of this world, but be transformed by the renewing of your mind. Then you will be able to test and approve what God's will is — his good, pleasing and perfect will. (NKJV)*

Developing and maintaining a Jesus-like perspective in leading others is both a challenge and a great adventure in experiencing *God's good, pleasing and perfect will.*

The Authors

ABOUT THE AUTHORS

Few have impacted the day-to-day management of people and companies more than Ken Blanchard. As a prominent author with over three dozen books including *The One Minute Manager*, speaker and business consultant, Ken is universally characterized as one of the most insightful, powerful and compassionate men in business today. Speaking from the heart with warmth and humor, he is a polished storyteller who makes the seemingly complex easy to understand.

KEN BLANCHARD

With a personal faith in Jesus Christ, Ken recognizes and lifts up Jesus as the greatest leadership role model of all time. He co-founded The Center for Faithwalk Leadership, now known as *Lead Like Jesus*, in 1999 with a mission "to glorify God by inspiring and equipping people to lead like Jesus."

Ken, his wife, Margie, two adult children, and three grandchildren live in Southern California. He is the co-founder, with his wife, Margie, and Chief Spiritual Officer of the Ken Blanchard Companies. With a Ph.D. from Cornell University, he has been a college professor, an imaginative entrepreneur, and a much sought after business guru. He is an avid golfer and a friend to many!

Phil Hodges, co-founder of *Lead Like Jesus*, served as a human resource and industrial relations manager in corporate America for 36 years with Xerox Corporation and U.S. Steel. In 1997, he served as a Consulting Partner with The Ken Blanchard Companies where he had responsibilities in leadership and customer service programs.

PHIL HODGES

In addition to helping leaders of faith walk their talk in the marketplace, Phil developed a passion for bringing effective leadership principles into the church when he served as member and chairman of his local church elder council for more than ten years. Phil finds great joy in his life-role relationships as husband, father and grandpa.

In 1999, Phil co-founded *Lead Like Jesus* whose mission is "to glorify God by inspiring and equipping people to Lead Like Jesus." He is the co-author of five books including *Lead Like Jesus: Lessons from the Greatest Leadership Role Model of All Time* and *The Most Loving Place in Town: A Modern Day Parable for the Church*, with Ken Blanchard. Phil and his wife, Jane Kinnaird Hodges, live in southern California where they are involved daily in their happiest season of influence as parents and grandparents in their expanding family.

STEVE D. GARDNER

A writer and corporate trainer investing in leaders with a dream team of collaborators at Ambassador Enterprises in Fort Wayne, IN are just a few things Steve does day to day. After graduation from Wheaton College, he and his wife, Maria, spent 28 years touring five continents in a music ministry that included writing and recording 16 albums.

As vice-president of Emerging Young Leaders, Steve began writing and editing leadership mentoring books including *Successful Youth Mentoring* (Volumes I and II) and *Lead On*. He has since written curricula used around the world by Crown Financial Ministries and has either ghosted or assisted in the writing of approximately 20 books.

A lover of tennis, skiing and scuba, Steve tells Ken he's saving golf for his golden years. In the meantime, he and Maria enjoy performing occasional concerts and spending time with their three grandchildren.

LOOKING FOR YOUR
NEXT STEPS?

CEO or teacher, pastor or parent, shopkeeper or student —
if you desire to impact the lives of others by leading like Jesus,
we invite you to join the LLJ movement and expand your leadership
abilities. Lead Like Jesus offers leadership-building resources for
teens and young adults as well as for seasoned executives, all
with the goal of demonstrating God's love for people while
helping them change the way they live, love, and lead.

The following products are available for purchase at
www.LeadLikeJesus.com

Sign up to receive the
E-DEVOTION

You can receive a new Lead Like Jesus de-
votional three times a week in your inbox!
These brief, insightful and challenging
reflections will help you
lead more like Jesus. Sign up at
www.LeadLikeJesus.com today!

Participate in a
High-Impact Workshop
ATTEND AN ENCOUNTER

An interactive program,
Encounter helps leaders
create positive change in
both their personal and
professional relationships.

Continue Your Personal
Growth by purchasing
LLJ STUDY GUIDES

Containing personal reflections, memory
verses, prayers, activities, and guidelines
for creating your own leadership plan.
These study guides contain lessons for
anyone who aspires to lead like Jesus.

Increase your Personal
Growth through
Accelerate™

Accelerate™ combines written
content, video, and powerful
questions to foster continued
growth as a LLJ leader. An
online program delivered daily
and built to move at a speed
that's right for you.

Engage the Next Generation through
STUDENT RESOURCES

Learning to lead like Jesus is an ongoing
pursuit. LLJ materials for students are
designed to foster life-changing leadership
habits and develop skills
early that will last a lifetime.

LEAD LIKE JESUS

NOTES

NOTES